W9-BQX-484

日本の一年

A Year in Japan

Kate T. Williamson

Princeton Architectural Press, New York

Published by
Princeton Architectural Press
37 East Seventh Street
New York, New York 10003

For a free catalog of books, call
1.800.722.6657.
Visit our web site at www.papress.com.

©2006 Kate T. Williamson
All rights reserved
Printed and bound in China
09 08 07 06   4 3 2 1 First edition

No part of this book may be used or repro-
duced in any manner without written permission
from the publisher, except in the context of
reviews.

Design: Kate T. Williamson
Editing: Clare Jacobson
Production: Dorothy Ball
Cover design: Deb Wood

Special thanks to: Nettie Aljian, Nicola
Bednarek, Janet Behning, Penny (Yuen Pik) Chu,
Russell Fernandez, Jan Haux, John King, Mark
Lamster, Nancy Eklund Later, Linda Lee,
Katharine Myers, Lauren Nelson, Jane Sheinman,
Scott Tennent, Jennifer Thompson, and Joseph
Weston of Princeton Architectural Press
—Kevin C. Lippert, publisher

The translation of the Minamoto Nobuakira
poem on page 36 is taken from *Gosenshū* 103 in
Murasaki Shikibu, *The Tale of Genji*, trans. with
an introd. by Edward G. Seidensticker (New
York: Vintage Books, 1990), 301n.

Library of Congress Cataloging-in-Publication Data
Williamson, Kate T. (Kate Tower), 1979–
   A year in Japan / Kate T. Williamson.
      p. cm.
   ISBN 1-56898-540-1 (alk. paper)
   1. Williamson, Kate T. (Kate Tower), 1979—
Themes, motives. 2. Japan—In art. 3. Japan—
Description and travel. I. Title.
   ND1839.W54A4 2006
   759.13—dc22
                              2005010828

*for my grandfather, James A. Williamson, Sr.,
who first talked to me about Japan*

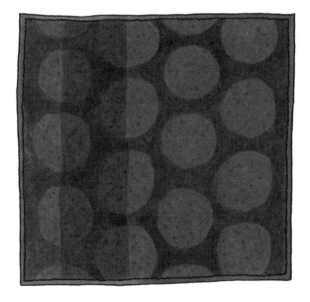

BEAUTY & WASHCLOTHS

As soon as I walked out of the train station on my
first day in Kyoto, I knew that I would love Japan.
I passed the ground floor of a department store on
my way to the street. To my right, next to purses and
scarves, was a wall of color and pattern — windowpane
plaid, polka dots, orange and turquoise, red and
magenta, lime and navy. Upon closer inspection, I
realized it was a display of washcloths, the most
beautiful washcloths I had ever seen. Unlike their
American counterparts, usually relegated to some
fourth-floor linen department and confined to
neutral bathroom hues, these squares of terry are not
used for washing but are kept in purses for drying
one's hands in public restrooms.

The washcloths were my first exposure to the attention to detail that characterizes much of Japan— both visually and socially. I soon came to realize just how much thought lies behind appearances and actions there, and that these details of beauty and nuances of word and deed are both expected and appreciated.

persimmons (kaki)

KEITAI

My cell phone (keitai) was lightweight, pearlescent, and pink. The highlight of this model, however, was the animated man who, at times, danced across the screen in a top hat, toasted marshmallows, went ice-fishing, popped bottles of champagne, or picnicked under cherry trees with his lady friend. He often made a pouting face when I turned off my phone.

All Japanese cell phones come with a cord (called a strappu) that serves as a hand strap. Most businessmen use the staid cord included with the phone, but for others the strappu is an opportunity for self-expression. Cords often commemorate vacations, friendships, or favorite animals; they usually involve bells. My strappu came from Okinawa and features a goya, an Okinawan vegetable.

BICYCLES

Kyoto is flat and populated by courteous motorists — the perfect cycling city. Bike-riding on Kyoto sidewalks is permitted and encouraged. Wide sidewalks often have a designated bike lane, and bikes seem to be allowed on smaller sidewalks as well. This takes some getting used to as a pedestrian. Most bikes come equipped with bells, and most courteous cyclists will ring these in advance, but I was never sure of the protocol. Was I supposed to move? Freeze? I was never certain, but, once I joined the ranks of the cyclists, I found the bell quite effective at parting all but the most obstinate groups of pedestrians.

The sidewalks are not, however, without hazards. I was in constant fear of accidentally cycling into an underground mall or subway entrance. I was also rather alarmed by the fact that, with the exception of foreign missionaries and the occasional professional-looking cyclist, absolutely no one—not kids, not elderly riders, not toddlers in seats mounted on their mothers' bikes—wore helmets. (Remarkably, in one year of cycling, I did not witness a single bike accident.)

The only difficulty in owning a bike in Kyoto is the shortage of legal places to park. Most areas outside subways and stores—basically everywhere—have signs prohibiting bicycles, and there is a roving flatbed truck that routinely impounds illegally parked bikes and motor scooters. They can be reclaimed for a fee, but I found this lurking danger a bit unsettling and never left my bike out of sight for long.

WAGASHI

Stores change the shapes and colors of wagashi, traditional Japanese sweets, each season— and often within a season—to reflect nature. This box, with wagashi in the form of ginko leaves, maple leaves that have not yet turned orange, and rice ready to be harvested, is sold in early autumn.

MATCHA

Upon arriving in any home, office, or art
gallery, one is almost always welcomed with
a cup of green tea and, often, an accompanying
piece of wagashi. I am particularly fond of
matcha, a powdered green tea used in tea
ceremonies and whipped into a froth with a small
bamboo whisk. Before drinking the somewhat bitter
matcha, one eats a piece of wagashi, either the molded
sugar variety or a beautiful bean paste confection.
The residual sweetness of the wagashi lingers on the
tongue and is meant to sweeten the matcha, which
should be consumed in several swallows.

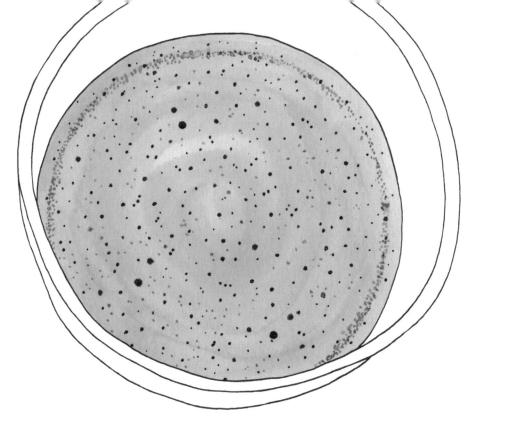

KOKE-DERA

The garden of Kyoto's Saihō-ji Temple, popularly known as Koke-dera (the Moss Temple) and designed by Musō Kokushi in 1339, is one of the most beautiful sights in Kyoto as well as one of the most difficult to visit.

A week after sending a postcard to the temple, I received a response stating the date and time I would be admitted. Twenty minutes before the appointed hour, I joined a group assembled outside the temple gates. A man appeared from inside and collected our postcards. We followed him to the lobby of the main hall, where we each made a mandatory donation of $30. We then entered a large room filled with small, low desks. Near each desk was a brush and ink set and a Buddhist sutra written in Japanese. I gathered from watching my fellow visitors that I was supposed to trace the sutra.

I started out very slowly, trying to make my characters conform as closely as possible to the lightly printed ones on the paper, but as the other scribes—all Japanese—began getting up one by one to hand in their sutras and tour the garden, I tried to pick up the pace. At long last, nearly an hour after I had started and with only five of the initial forty people remaining, I finished the final strokes of the last character and was able to see the garden, which was, in fact, well worth the effort.

SHOJIN RYORI

Kyoto is home to a number of temples that serve shōjin ryōri, the vegetarian cuisine of Zen Buddhist monks. Using fresh vegetables and avoiding strong seasonings, the shōjin ryōri chef aims to balance the six "flavors" of bitter, sour, sweet, salty, hot, and light. The version served to temple guests is rather expensive but exquisite (and quite filling). Sitting on a tatami mat in a room overlooking Tenryū-ji Temple's garden in late November, I ordered the "yuki" (snow) lunch.

1. Green tea
2. Cold assortment including a soft chestnut, fu (wheat gluten) in the shape of a maple leaf, tofu wrapped in greens, konnyaku (pulverized roots that have been reconstituted in a rubbery form), and a bowl of sweet beans
3. Cold greens and small mushrooms
4. Cold goma dōfu (creamy, sesame-based "tofu") with a dab of wasabi on top
5. Part of a very ripe persimmon and two perfect grapes with the bottoms sliced off for easy peeling (grapes are peeled in Japan, as are most fruits with skin)
6. Rice
7. Hot tofu and yuba (a tofu by-product that is skimmed off the top) in a light broth
8. Tsukemono (pickled vegetables)
9. Mushroom-flavored miso soup with tofu
10. Hot tofu in a syrupy sauce

maple leaves (momiji)

I bought this boxed lunch (o-bentō) whenever I went on a long train trip

SHINKANSEN

The first time I rode the bullet train (shinkansen),
I expected to feel my hair blowing in the wind and
the flesh of my face wobbling from the speed, but the
train was oddly quiet and serene as it moved past
rice fields and through mountains. I had prepared
for the speed of light, but the shinkansen seemed to
be moving more at the speed of really fast. With the
exception of the conductor's announcements and the
occasional shouts of attendants pushing food and
gift carts up and down the aisles, there was a strange
stillness and muting of sounds in the train, as
though I were traveling to Tokyo in an hermetically
sealed spaceship that had reached cruising altitude.

If only I could show them to someone who knows,
This moon, these flowers, this night that should not be wasted.

— Minamoto nobuakira

MOON-VIEWING

One of my favorite aspects of Japanese culture is
the combination of nature appreciation and social
events. There are maple-viewing expeditions,
evening parties under the cherry blossoms, and,
although this seems to have been more common
in earlier times, moon-viewing parties. Many old
aristocratic residences have special platforms or
rooms where nobles would gather to write moon-
related verse as they gazed at the sky or into the
moon's reflection in a nearby pond.

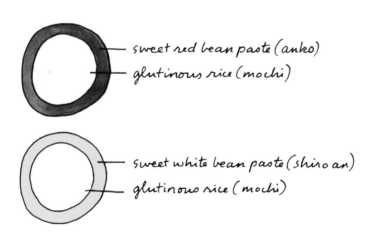

sweet red bean paste (anko)
glutinous rice (mochi)

sweet white bean paste (shiro an)
glutinous rice (mochi)

tsukimi dango, sweets made especially for moon-viewing

In Japan, people look for a rabbit in the moon (tsuki no usagi)

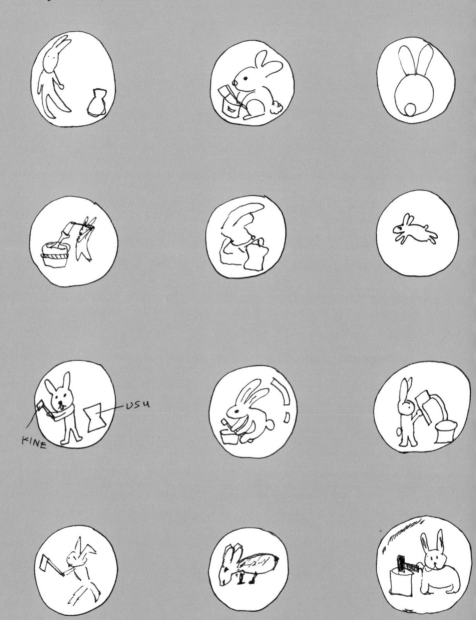

KINE
USU

who is pounding rice into mochi (glutinous rice).

I was surprised to discover that everyone does not see the same one.

Nicely Nicely Johnson

TAKARAZUKA

I have seen the future of theater, and it is <u>Guys and Dolls</u> performed in Japanese by an all-female cast.

<u>Guys and Dolls</u> is just one of the many theatrical offerings of the Takarazuka Revue Company, a theater created in 1914 in the town of Takarazuka by railroad tycoon Ichizo Kobayashi. His vision of the "theater of the future," the company is comprised entirely of women and devoted to performing modern, Broadway-style musicals in Japanese. (<u>West Side Story</u> premiered in Japan as a Takarazuka performance in 1968.)

After weeks of seeing posters on the subway, I decided that I needed to see <u>Guys and Dolls</u>. I arrived at the Takarazuka Grand Theater for a matinee and found myself surrounded by middle-aged ladies. We processed past several souvenir shops (one called

"Rococo" specialized in rhinestone jewelry and fans) into a very pink lobby, where an automated grand piano was playing the _Guys and Dolls_ overture. Beyond the lobby was an enormous theater filled with more women and about fifteen dutiful husbands.

Aside from "crap-u game-u," I could understand very little, but, since I had some familiarity with the English version, I was able to follow along. The highlight of the performance came after the official end of the musical: the cast bowed, the curtain went down, and then the curtain went back up to reveal a Vegas-style stage set. Wearing elaborate costumes — often involving ostrich feathers — each of the leads took her turn singing a disco-style reprise as the crowd applauded with great enthusiasm.

Bananas often come sealed in a plastic bag.

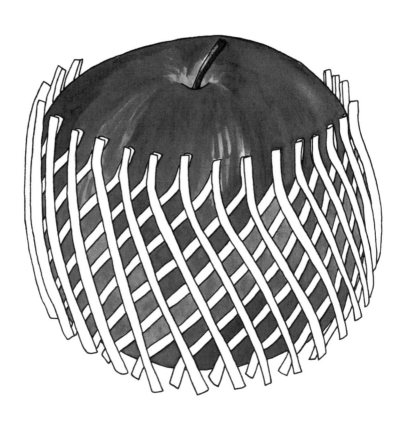

SAFE FRUIT

Japanese apples tend to be enormous, expensive, and well-protected. I once bought an apple in a department store supermarket (most department stores have supermarkets on the lowest level), and before I could stammer something about not needing a bag, the apple was surrounded by a foam cozy and placed inside a paper bag, which was then sealed with a sticker bearing the department store's name and handed to me in a plastic shopping bag.

washi (paper)

SANTAFUL WORLD

Christmas in Japan is a largely secular and commercial holiday that has come to resemble Valentine's Day (Christmas Eve is a very big date night). I began seeing ads in September for Christmas Eve dinner, concert, and hotel room packages. By November, a giant artificial tree had been erected in Kyoto Station, and one floor of a department store had been transformed into "Santaful World," a Christmas retail center whose merchandise included a dancing Scooby Doo dressed as Santa Claus.

Each year, Kentucky Fried Chicken offers special Christmas chicken platters and outfits the fiberglass Colonel outside the store in a Santa costume. The major food associated with Christmas in Japan, however, is Christmas cake (Kurisumasu kēki), which resembles strawberry shortcake with some plastic holly or Santa decorations on top.

New Year's mochi are displayed in front of the household shrine.

O-SHOGATSU

In contrast to Christmas, the coming of the new year (O-Shogatsu) is a very important family holiday; most of the nation shuts down for several days as people return to their hometowns. On New Year's Eve, a family usually goes to a nearby Buddhist temple to hear the temple bell struck 108 times — once for each of the 108 Buddhist sins — at or just before midnight. Shinto shrines are generally visited on New Year's Day, but some are also popular New Year's Eve destinations.

I waited for the year to change amid an orderly throng at Kyoto's Yasaka Shrine. There was none of the noise or rowdiness I associate with an American New Year's Eve; in fact, I might not have even known that midnight was approaching had it not been for a small group of young men counting down behind me. As if on cue, however, the crowd began to toss coins towards the shrine as soon as the new year had officially begun. (Policemen stationed near the front of the shrine wore clear plastic face guards to protect them from errant throws.) I shuffled along in the now-moving mass until I was deposited in a lane lined with food stalls. I bought a candied apple.

I found this electric rug (hotto hapetto) in my closet.

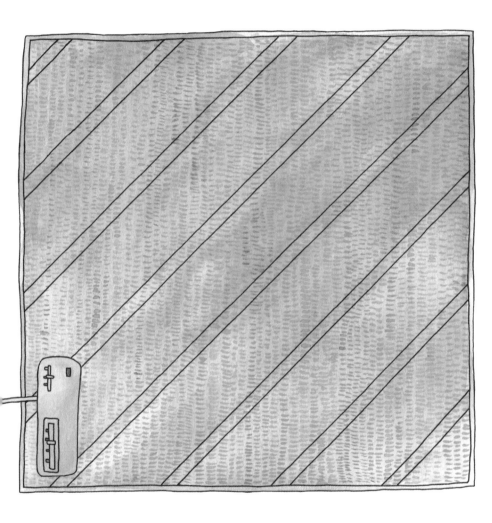

ON BEING COLD

I have never in my life been as cold as I was the winter I spent in Kyoto, but it is not because Kyoto is actually that cold. There is a general lack of central heating in Japan, and many buildings, apparently including mine, were built without insulation. This perpetual chill has inspired many novel warming devices: heaters implanted in the middle of tables (kotatsu), electric heating "fans," and heating pouches worn under clothing.

When I moved into my apartment, I found a large box on the top shelf of my closet containing a small, square rug with a cord on one end. I learned from my neighbor that this was an electric rug (hotto kāpetto). As I was not entirely sure of its provenance and I had a slight fear of electrocution, I was initially reluctant to plug it in; by January, however, it had become so cold that I decided it was worth the risk. It was surprisingly effective, and, from that day forth, the hot carpet was the center of all activity.

Meoto-Iwa (the Wedded Rocks), Futami-ga-Ura

A sacred rope (shimenawa) unites the "male" and "female" rocks of Meoto-Iwa, a sacred Shinto site. The shimenawa is replaced in a ceremony three times a year, and extra pieces of rope are given to patient spectators.

STAMP RALLY

Rubber stamps (often chained to a table) and stamp pads (often somewhat dry) are available for making souvenirs at nearly every public place. Museums, train stations, and famous temples and shrines in particular can be relied upon to have a stamping station in some corner, usually labeled with a sign that says "Stamp Rally" and stocked with sheets of white paper.

市立
博物館

都市

道新記念

TOKYO
東京

大地より通山そして信仰への旅

JR紀伊勝浦駅

京・津・奈スタンプラリー

盧山寺

文学ゆかりの地

河口湖

角堂

高松塚壁画館 入館記念

IRIOMOTE ISLA

English is frequently used on Japanese products.

Happy infinite romances occur in a newborn oasis. Wink your future.

elastic
today

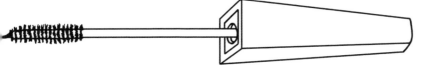

navel hair design

navel is the hair doctor.
we design your hair with less damage.

(on the door of a hair salon)

INTERNATIONAL LETTER WRITING WEEK 国際文通週間 1998

SPARKLY LADIES

There is a contingent of middle-aged to elderly Japanese women who like to sparkle and no shortage of stores that carry sparkly merchandise. These ladies — wives, mothers, grandmothers — have no qualms about wearing sequins by day or, interestingly, dyeing their graying hair a variety of colorful shades. It is not unusual to see a woman in her sixties in a green, purple, or electric blue sweater set (often with rhinestone detailing on the collar and sleeves) with matching hair. There appears to be nothing countercultural about this.

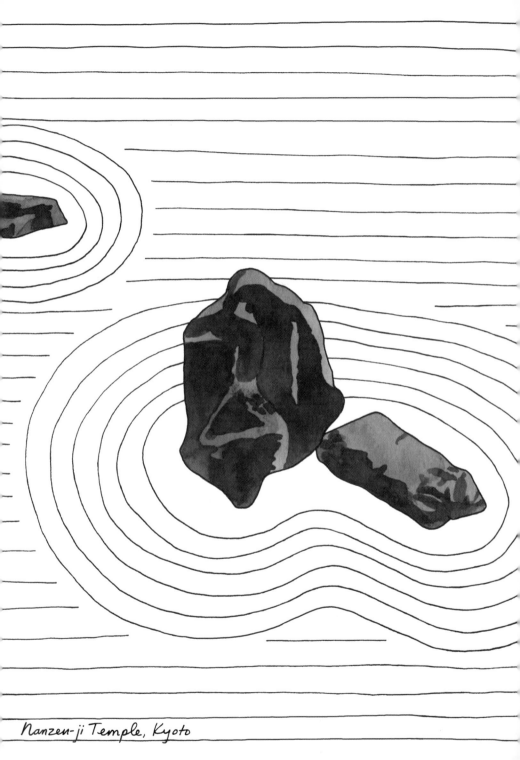

Nanzen-ji Temple, Kyoto

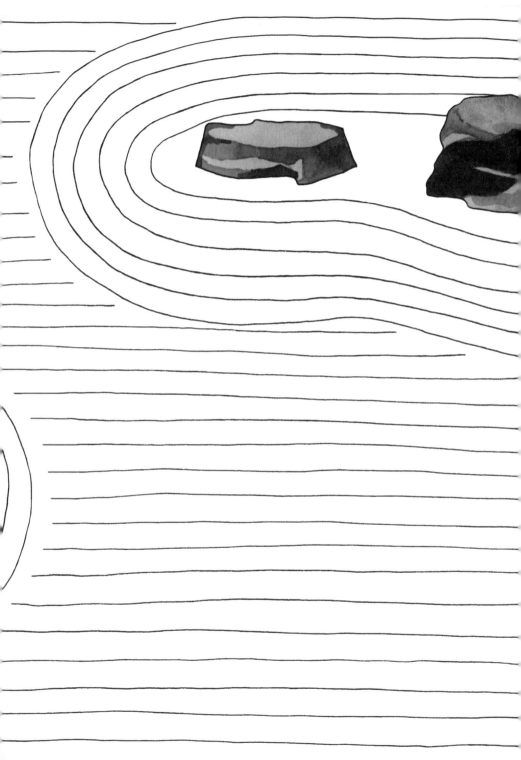

ZEN & THE MOVIES

The first time I attempted to practice zazen, a form of seated meditation, the Zen master at Kyoto's Ryōzen-an Temple instructed me to lower my eyes but warned against closing them completely. Pointing to his eyelids, he said, "They are like movie screens."

Afterwards, talking over tea, he mentioned that in his youth he often went to the movies in his free time. Though he enjoyed the images he saw in the theater, they proved quite distracting during his evening meditation. He started watching two movies a day and discovered that they canceled each other out.

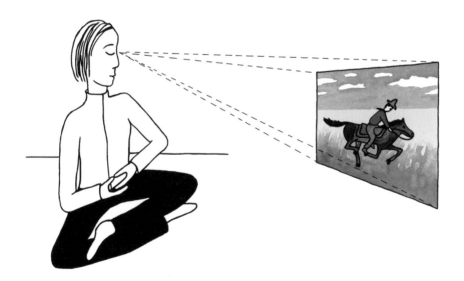

Soy sauce for takeout sus

usually comes in a small plastic fish.

bamboo lounge, Futami-ga-Ura

KARAOKE:
THE IMPORTANCE OF BEING EARNEST

Although karaoke bars exist in Japan, much singing occurs in box-style karaoke establishments. For a low hourly rate (especially before the peak hours of 11 p.m. to 4 a.m.) a small group can rent a private room equipped with a television, two microphones, speakers, and a revolving light system. Tambourines may be requested for no additional charge.

Japanese karaoke singers tend to be quite earnest and take the performance of signature songs (o-haho) very seriously. I had performed Prince's "Raspberry Beret" several times at home and, during my Japanese debut, was relieved to discover that this song (albeit slightly disguised as "Raspberry Ballet") was available. I could never find it again, however, and I was left to choose from the nearly complete works of the Beatles, ABBA, the Carpenters, Elton John, Madonna, and, oddly, Scatman John. It did not take long for Elton John's "Your Song" to become my signature song.

A caveat: Avoid the songs of Mariah Carey and Whitney Houston at all costs unless you are very, very good. (More than once, flying high after a successful "Your Song," I had to abort "How Will I Know" after thirty seconds and then apologize to my audience.)

plum blossoms (ume no hana)

ON DISCRETION or JAPAN:
A THIRTEEN-YEAR-OLD GIRL'S PARADISE

People in Japan are in general quite discreet. Many Western-style toilets, for example, have a button marked with a musical note that, when pressed, prompts a nearby speaker to emit the sound of a toilet flushing. When using a less-advanced commode, most women will strategically flush the toilet to mask any bathroom sounds and then flush again.

Modesty extends to the retail world as well. After ringing up female sanitary products in any supermarket or convenience store, the clerk will first wrap the purchase in a brown paper bag, seal it, and then place the package into the store's customary — and translucent — plastic bag.

Should you decide to try on clothing in Japan, you will encounter perhaps the most elaborate and complete system of coverage in the world. Dressing rooms are often circular and enveloped by heavy canvas or vinyl curtains that overlap by about a yard, making them challenging to exit.

← MAIKO

← apprentice

← real hair

← elaborate hair
accessories

colorful collar

GEISHA →

professional →

wig →

white collar →

LUNCH WITH A GEISHA

One day as I was leaving a guest house in Kyoto, the owner, Tani-san, invited me to have lunch with him and his friend Haruno, a geisha. Tani-san met her about ten years ago at a Kyoto tea house and is a great admirer. (I later noticed several posters of her in the lobby of the guest house.) Haruno-san now runs her own tea house and was, according to Tani-san, the first geisha to be signed by Columbia Records. She is also a television, newspaper, and radio personality.

We waited at Haruno-san's house for about ten minutes before she emerged wearing a white button-down shirt, a long denim skirt, and black sneakers. She wore little makeup, and her hair was pulled back into a short ponytail. Haruno-san is surprisingly tall—perhaps 5'8"—with small feet and very graceful hands. At first glance, she didn't seem that geisha-like in her civilian clothing, but, as we walked to the coffee shop, she moved as though she were wearing an invisible kimono. She ordered an egg sandwich and iced tea.

Over lunch, I learned that Haruno-san was born in Kyoto and became a maiko (an apprentice geisha) when she was fifteen. Her daughter, now fourteen, is taking dancing lessons and may or may not decide to become a maiko. Haruno-san works daily from about 6 p.m. to midnight, retires at about 2 a.m., and rises at 10 in the morning. After she finished her sandwich, Haruno-san lit a cigarette and took a picture of me with her cell phone. Tani-san bought ten posters and a CD from her.

TASTY CONVENIENCE

There are at least two convenience stores (konbini) per block in any metropolitan area. Although I often bought salads (surprisingly fresh) from konbini, my favorite foods involved rice or soy beans.

ohagi, a rice ball with red beans

mitarashi dango, glutinous rice balls in a sweet, soy-based sauce

natto, fermented soy beans with a pungent odor

There was something startling about seeing sumo
wrestlers in the traditional yukata (cotton kimono)
and geta (wooden clogs)

wearing headphones,
    making withdrawals at ATMs,
        riding the subway, and, once,
            drinking strawberry milk after a match.

peach blossoms (momo no hana)

GOLDEN VEINS

Cracks in ancient Japanese pottery—including the
occasional museum piece—are often repaired with
metallic "filling." (The cracks are first filled with
resin and then lacquered and coated with silver
or gold.) This work is done by a specialist, who
carefully considers the colors and feeling of a piece
before selecting the appropriate filling medium.
Accustomed to a culture where repairs aim to be
invisible, I was somewhat taken aback by this
decorative method that highlights the "imperfections."
A friend who collects pottery explained that the
piece becomes a different work of art after it is
repaired and that the golden veins create a
new sort of beauty.

bowl, Kamakura period (1185-1333), Miho Museum

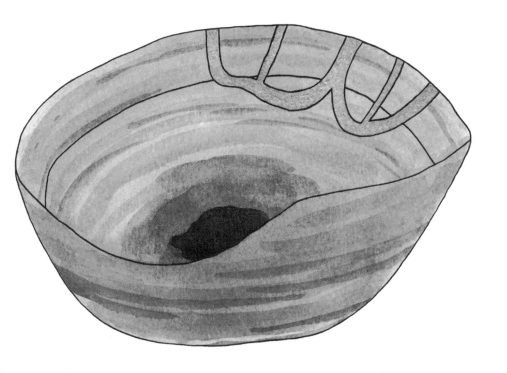

cherry blossoms (sakura)

EVANESCENCE & PHOTOGRAPHY

During the prime weeks of sakura season in April, the cherry blossom sites are swarming with tourists and locals alike, most of whom come bearing tripods and incredibly large and professional-looking cameras. The flowers are very beautiful, but part of their appeal lies in their fleeting existence. Blossoms can be admired for about a week before they flutter off the branches, and a strong wind or heavy rainstorm can prematurely scatter petals to the ground. Of course, the trees throughout the country are all on slightly different schedules, so it is possible to enjoy cherry blossoms for a month or so by traveling to higher altitudes (a project made easier by daily television reports charting the nationwide blooming progress).

Still, a sense of urgency permeates the cherry blossom season. Although I, too, did my best to capture the beauty of these flowers on film, I can't help but wonder if photography—trying to make a permanent image of an impermanent subject—isn't entirely contrary to the nature of sakura.

BOOK BAGS

Spring is the traditional time for beginning new jobs and school years in Japan, and, in the weeks leading up to April, the stores are filled with back-to-school merchandise and specials. Many displays feature book bags, especially the colorful and sturdy leather models (randoseru) carried by elementary school students. Priced between $200 and $450, these shockingly expensive school accessories are often gifts from grandparents and are built to last, at least until junior high, when they are replaced by cheaper cloth bags.

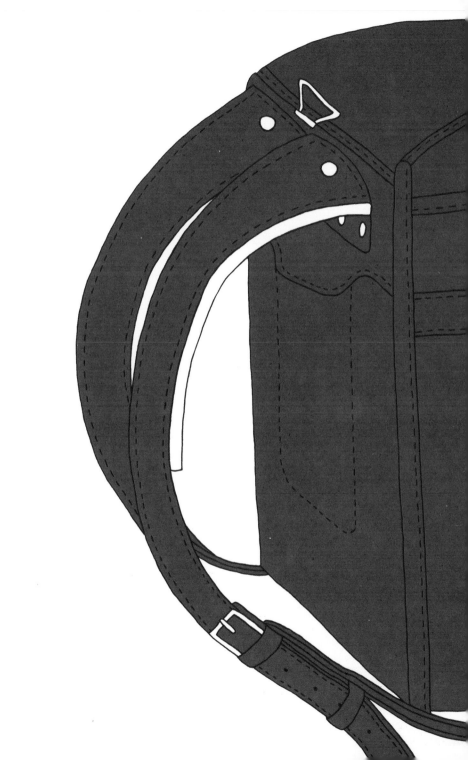

black

sepia

green

navy

ultramarine

yellow

orange

coral

red

pink

rose

wine

Japan is sock paradise. I have never seen so many

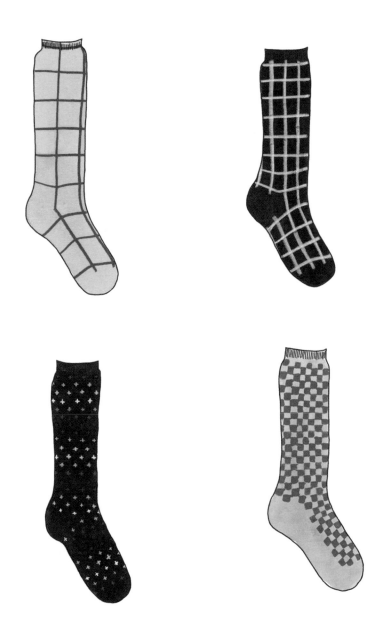

...eautiful socks or so many stores devoted entirely to them.

This advanced sock culture can be attributed in part to the

custom of removing one's shoes upon entering a home.

FUNKY MONKEY BABY

One Sunday as I was riding my bike down Kyoto's main street, I chanced upon a dozen men dancing in a circle on the flat, open plaza in front of the City Hall. Wearing blue jeans, stiff pompadours, and identical black T-shirts, they were taking turns in the center doing a hybrid sort of twisting and break-dancing to "Rock Around the Clock," which was blaring from a nearby generator-powered boombox.

I learned that they were members of the newly formed Kyoto Rockabilly Club (which has since become a chapter of the Tokyo Rockabilly Club) and are all, with few exceptions, temple carpenters who also happen to like dancing to rock 'n' roll. Ranging in age from twenty-one to thirty-five, these men meet every Sunday — rain or shine — from 1 to 6 p.m. and are accompanied by tapes that alternate between

American oldies and Japanese rock 'n' roll (including my personal favorite, "Funky Monkey Baby," a Japanese hit from the 70s). The dancers take occasional breaks for snacks, girlfriends, grooming, repairing their dance shoes with electrical tape (the surface of the plaza is very rough), and removing the occasional wayward ball or toddler from the center of the dance circle.

A little after six, when the music stops and night is falling, the dancers produce little brooms and dustpans and meticulously sweep up every particle of sole and electrical tape from the plaza. Then, amid a flurry of complicated handshakes, the dancers leave and the plaza is once again the realm of bureaucrats and dog walkers.

I flew to southern Okinawa and took a ferry to Taketomi Island.

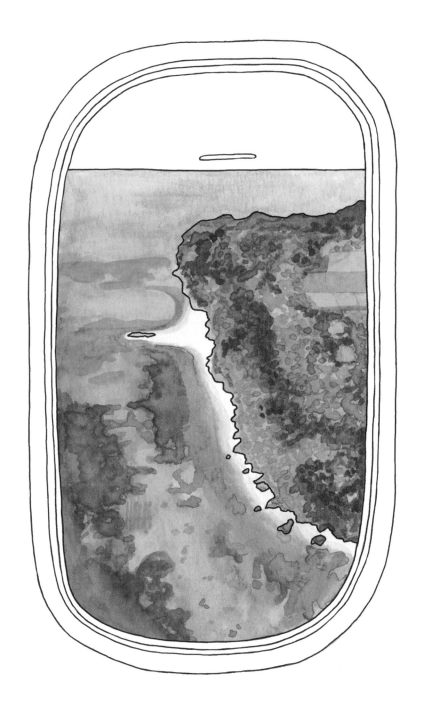

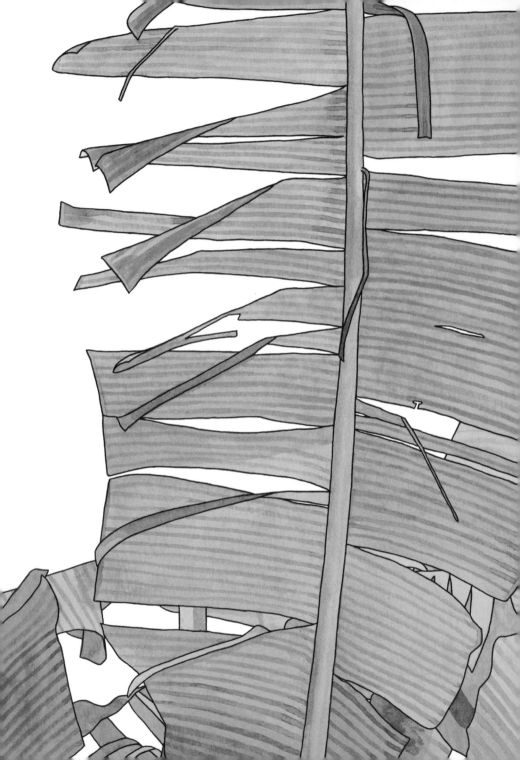

banana leaves

TAKETOMI-JIMA

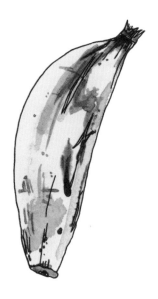

shima banana (actual size)

hot hibiscus juice

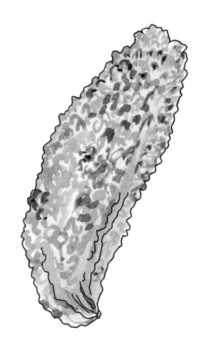

goya, a bitter vegetable

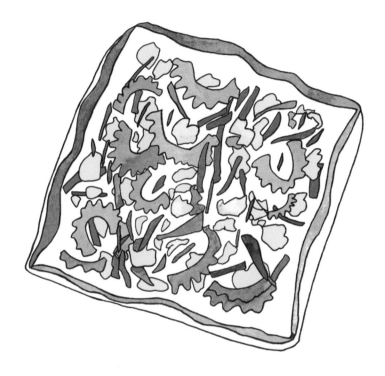

goya champuru, a local specialty

sanshin

Star-shaped sand (fossils)

real

Japanese taxis are quite elegant.

Nachi no taki, Japan's highest waterfall and a sacred Shinto site

One of my favorite places in Kyoto is Shisendō, a seventeenth-century mountain retreat built by the poet-hermit Ishikawa Jōzan. This sōzu (or shishi-odoshi) fills with water, tips, and then strikes the rock, making a clunking noise that keeps the deer away from the garden. I especially liked listening to the rush of water just before the bamboo hit the rock.

TSUYU

June marks the beginning of Japan's rainy season (tsuyu), which lasts until mid-July. This season brings not constant rain but rather sporadic showers almost every day. Consequently, the umbrella industry has flourished, giving rise to a large selection of high-priced, designer-licensed umbrellas that encroach on the handbags in the department stores each spring. A cheaper alternative, especially for those caught in unexpected storms, is the ubiquitous clear vinyl umbrella, available for the price of a sandwich at any convenience store. Even after the rainy season has ended, the umbrellas persist, usually in a frillier parasol version made of UV-blocking fabric.

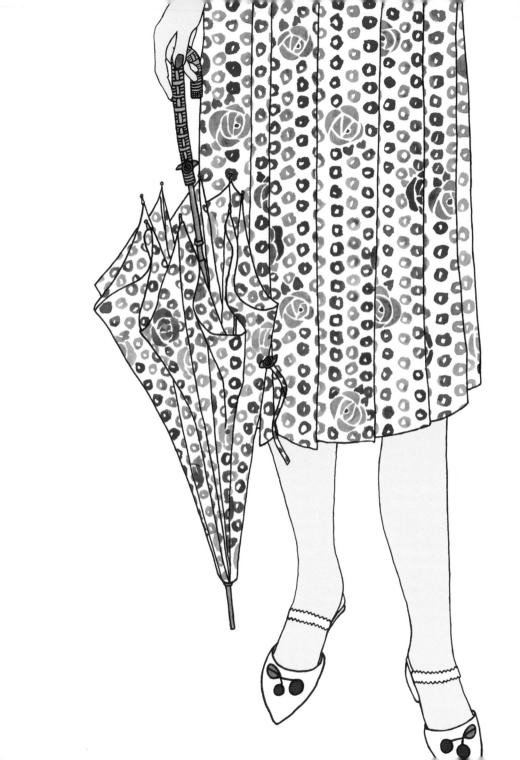

hydrangea (ajisai)

TOFU

Everyday at 12:20 pm, an elderly man came down my street in Kyoto pushing a small wooden cart as he rang a cowbell. Several other older men with carts made noises at other times of the day, and I had assumed that they were collecting boxes, sharpening knives, or offering some other service of limited appeal to me. One day when I happened to be in the street at 12:20 p.m., I was surprised and delighted to discover that this man was a tofu vendor whose cart contained blocks of tofu he had made that morning.

The Japanese language has a variety of counting words. There are different words for counting people, birds and rabbits, flat objects, and socks, among other things.

How to count up to seven blocks of tofu (when asked for more, my friend told me no one would order more than that):

1 block = itchō
2 blocks = nichō
3 blocks = sanchō
4 blocks = yonchō
5 blocks = gochō
6 blocks = rokuchō
7 blocks = nanachō

SHIBORIZOME

I studied shiborizome, a traditional textile art that uses sewing and indigo-dyeing to create subtle and beautiful patterns, with Hiroko Harada at her studio in Shinshiro (near Nagoya). She works exclusively with natural indigo harvested from the plants on Shikoku Island and kindly introduced me to some basic techniques.

My favorite design — partly because it requires no advanced sewing skills — is called "hotaru," which means "firefly." I attached natural cotton balls (the untreated cotton resists the indigo dye) tightly to both sides of a cotton cloth, dyed the cloth in the indigo, and then removed the cotton balls to reveal the "fireflies."

Shades of Indigo (Ai)

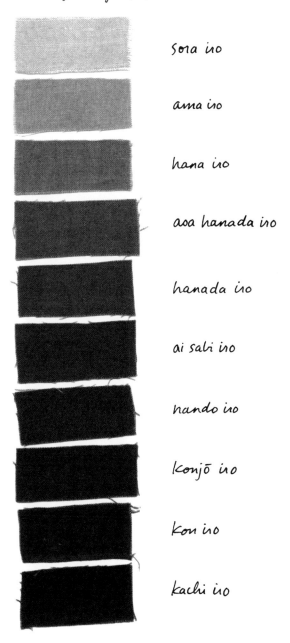

Sora iro

ama iro

hana iro

asa hanada iro

hanada iro

ai sabi iro

nando iro

Konjō iro

Kon iro

Kachi iro

willow (yanagi)

KAMO-GAWA

The shallow Kamo River (Kamo-gawa) runs south through Kyoto and is a prime gathering spot in warmer months. The Kamo draws to its banks — in addition to many cyclists, walkers, and young couples — a motley crew of aspiring performers. The close proximity of houses and apartments in Kyoto does not allow for much indoor practice, so on weekends and evenings the river becomes a venue for free performances (of varying levels).

On one particularly lively Saturday afternoon I passed a student practicing his tuba, three middle-aged men rehearsing a high-energy dance routine to "Barbie Girl," and two would-be bartenders attempting advanced maneuvers with tape-covered bottles.

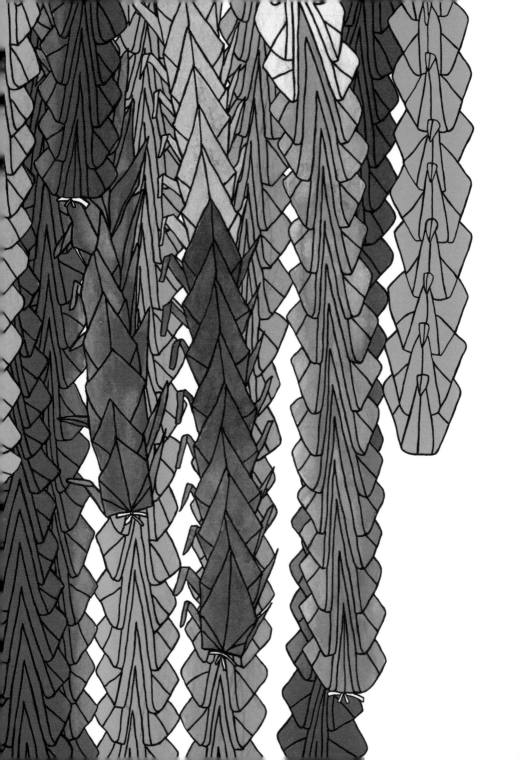

ONE THOUSAND PAPER CRANES

In Hiroshima's Peace Memorial Park there is a special children's memorial that recounts the true story of a young girl, Sadako, who was diagnosed with leukemia as a result of the radiation from the atomic bomb. Sadako tried to make one thousand paper cranes — a Japanese symbol of longevity — in the hope that she would recover. She did not live to finish her project, but her classmates folded the remaining cranes in her memory. Today the memorial and park grounds are adorned with garlands of thousands and thousands of paper cranes made by school children from Japan and throughout the world. A Japanese friend told me that every Japanese child knows how to fold a paper crane.

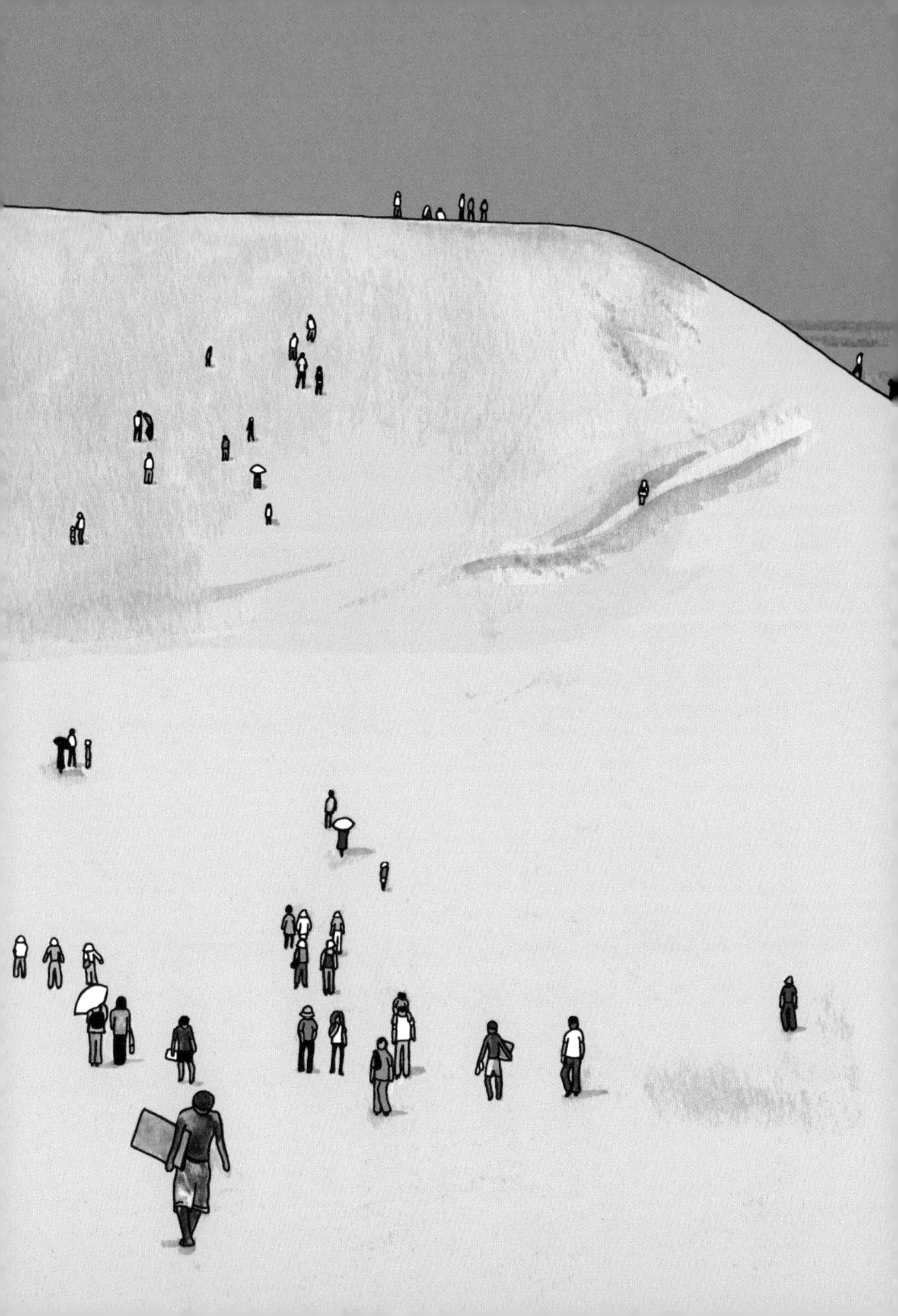

Tottori Sakyū (sand dunes), Tottori

Summer in Japan is marked by festivals, fireworks, and an array of cooling treats to eat. The circular fan (uchiwa) is a common and useful festival accessory and is tucked into the back of one's obi, the sash worn with a kimono, when not in use.

Milk kintoki ● shaved ice topped with sweet azuki bean

condensed milk, and balls of glutinous rice

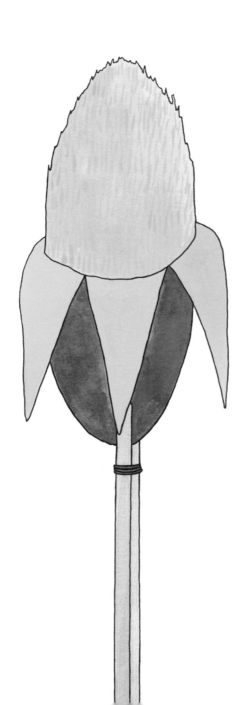

THE PERFECT MANGO-EATING METHOD

I bought a delicious mango from a food stall during Kyoto's Gion Festival. Cool, sweet, and not at all stringy, the mango was peeled half-way down and impaled by two chopsticks that were bound together by a rubber band. The mango stayed secure, and I did not get sticky.

The Japanese word for fireworks is "hanabi," which means "fire flower."

LIGHT-UPS

Many Kyoto temples offer evening "light-up" displays that use carefully positioned, high-powered lights to illuminate the maple leaves or cherry blossoms on their grounds. I had visited an illuminated temple in the fall, and, although the translucent leaves were dramatic and somewhat interesting, I had no desire to view cherry blossoms under 1000-watt lights in the spring.

By the end of summer, however, I had begun to let down my guard. A component of O-bon, an important holiday honoring ancestors in mid-August, is the illumination of temples and graveyards. Glowing lanterns sounded quite beautiful and certainly much less artificial than the light-ups of spring and fall. Lured by the promise of 2000 lanterns, I went

to the mountain-top temple of Enryaku-ji.
(In retrospect, perhaps the revolving disco ball hung
amid the pine trees by the temple's entrance
should have given me an indication of what was
to come.)

As I approached the main, seventeenth-century
building, there were indeed lanterns lining the
walkway. These lanterns were nearly
overpowered, however, by the giant red and
green spotlights trained on the ancient trees above
them. Inside the temple courtyard, monks awash
in magenta, orange, green, and red light moved
about solemnly as a young man wearing a black
T-shirt with "Event" printed on the back shoveled
dry ice into a smoke machine.

AWA ODORI

From the 12th to the 15th of August, thousands of men, women, and children dance in the streets of Tokushima (on Shikoku Island) for the Awa Odori, an annual dance festival that occurs during O-bon. As large groups of dancers move in tight synchronization to the accompaniment of drums and flutes, they chant:

Odoru ahō ni
Miru ahō
Onaji aho nara
Odorana son son!

You're a fool to dance,
A fool to watch,
Well, if you're a fool either way,
What a loss not to dance, a loss, a loss!

lotus (hasu)

DAIMONJI

Every year on August 16th, five giant bonfires in various forms—a boat, a torii gate, and three Chinese characters of Buddhist significance—are lit on the hillsides of Kyoto. The dai character (which means "great") is visible year-round on the side of Mt. Daimonji, but it is illuminated only on this one evening. The fires are intended to lead the spirits of the ancestors back to the realm of the dead at the conclusion of O-bon. I watched from the roof of my apartment until the last embers burned out.

DOMO ARIGATO GOZAIMASU

I am very grateful to my grandmother Dorothy Williamson, my parents Judy & Jim Williamson, Yukiko & Wataru Ishihara, Toshi Morikawa, Chiho Ito, and Hiroko Harada for their great assistance and encouragement. I am especially grateful for the George Peabody Gardner Traveling Fellowship, which gave me the opportunity to spend a year in Japan. I would also like to thank Clare Jacobson and Princeton Architectural Press for giving me the chance to bring this book to fruition and for the very helpful suggestions and support.

Thank you:

Linas Alsenas; Joan & David Andrews; Kiyoko & Nobuyuki Aoki; Mitsuyo & Shinya Aoki; Constance Arauz; Jenny Beem; Randy Bell; Max Bernstein; Vanessa Bertozzi; Owen Bossola; Pau Corral; Alejandro Correa; Marci Cressman; Suzy & Larry Daniels; David Michael DiGregorio; Kathryn Dunton; Anne Estes; Phyllis French; the Frownfelter Family; Emiko & Hiroshi Fujimori; Bob Gardner; Kimberley Gatrell; Alfred Guzzetti; Mary Halpenny-Killip; Naomi & Takaaki Harada; Ramie Ho; Susan Homer; Yoshisuke, Kei, & Mei Ito; Akihiro Itoh; Stephanie Kahn; Rose Kakoza; Kazuhiko Kaneda; Noriyuki Kato; Kuniko Katsuyama; Chris Killip; Rachel Korner; the Kreider Family; the Kuhn Family; Kyoto Rockabilly Club; Anna Laufersweiler;

Tanya Leiby; Mary & Steve Lieberman; Yuko & Andrew Lewandowski; Kattia Marquez; Shigeiharu, Tomoko & Yuka Maruyama; Mike Miller; Ryoko Mishima; Nancy M. Mitchnick; Kumiko Miura; Annie & Tom Moll; Clifton Monteith; Robb Moss; Ayano Ninomiya; Reiko, Naomasa, & Junko Ochi; Karen Palcho; Queena Pasko; Sarah Peter; Skip Phinney; Adele Pressman; Celia Pym; the Ratz Family; Heather Schwartz; Kimiko & Richard Steiner; Marjie Thompson-Longshore; Cecile & Bruce Wiegand; Mildred Willenbrock; Richie Williams; Jan Williamson; Peggy & John Woodward; Ching Han Wong; Therese Workman; Nukumi & Daisuke Yamate; Mikio Yasaka; Britt & Hiroshi Yoda; Hiroshi Yoshikatsu; Alison Zacharias; and Elizabeth Zacharias

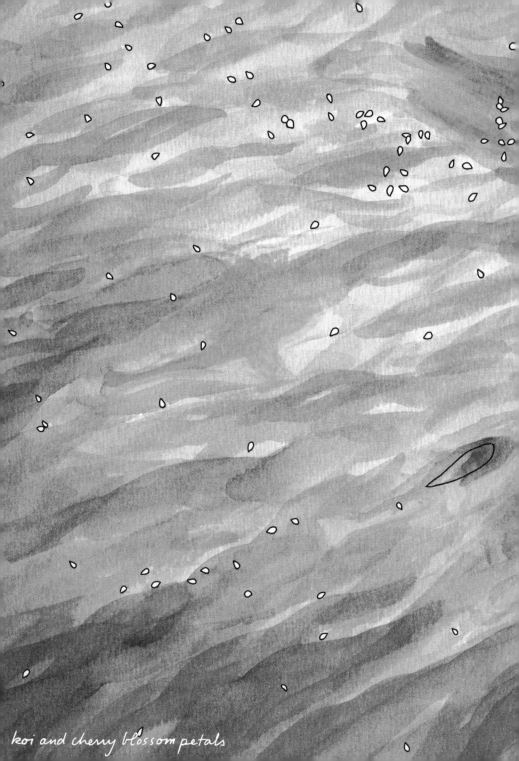

koi and cherry blossom petals